LIGHT IN THE MOURNING

by

Evelyn Taylor-McNamara

The Tennessee Pulishing House
Mosheim, Tennessee
August 2009
First Edition

Blessings,
Evelyn
Romans 8:28

LIGHT IN THE MOURNING

by

Evelyn Taylor-McNamara

PUBLISHED IN THE UNITED STATES OF AMERICA
BY
The Tennessee Publishing House
496 Mountain View Drive
Mosheim, TN 37818

Cover Design
by
Kellie Warren-Underwood

All Scriptures are taken from the King James Version (KJV) of the Holy Bible.

Disclaimer
This document is an original work of the author. It may include reference to information commonly known or freely available to the general public. Any resemblance to his published information is purely coincidental. The author has in no way attempted to use material not of her own origination. Black Forest Press disclaims any association with or responsibility for the ideas, opinions or facts as expressed by the author of this book. No dialogue is totally accurate or precise.

Printed in the United States of America
Library of Congress
Catalogue-in-Publication

ISBN: 978-1-58275-211-2

Acknowledgements

With thanks to my family and friends for the prayerful encouragement and love given to me after my husband's death and my son's kidnapping. I could not have found the strength to move on with my life without my faith in God and support of my family.

I am particularly grateful to Shirly Garvais for her contribution in making this book possible. It was her vision and insistence that God wanted me to use my story for His glory.

A special thanks to Cherie Nash for her support and encouragement. She was always there to walk beside me, lifting my spirits, during my most difficult hours.

Foreword

I knew of Evelyn Taylor-Mcnamara long before I had the privilege of knowing her. Knowing her has been a blessing to my life and the life of my family as I have had the honor of being her pastor for the last seven years.

She has not allowed her life to be defined by adversity or success. She has allowed her life to be an example of God at work in all circumstances. I believe you will be challenged, comforted, and possibly even convicted, as you read of an ordinary life lived in an extraordinary manner because of her daily walk and personal relationship with the Lord.

May God bless you as you see how he can work through your adversities to bring about good. ***Romans 8:28 (KJV)*** reads *"And we know that all things work together for good to them that love God, to them who are the called according to His purpose."* It certainly has been true in Evelyn's life. May it be so in yours as well.

Charles L. Harkleroad, Pastor
Leadvale Missionary Baptist Church
874 Leadvale Church Road
White Pine, Tennessee 37890
July 2009

Publisher's Note

As a book publisher for over 18 years, and having published over 1,670 decent books by 850 authors, during that time period, there are only four other books about which I have personally made professional comment. *Light In The Mourning* is one of those books.

I suggest you carefully and slowly devour each page, digesting it with an open and unassuming mind. Not expecting what you will read may catch you off guard, but you will be bolstered in your Christian life by how Evelyn Taylor-McNamara has displayed a unique ability to cope with doorstep disaster, not once, but twice within a matter of a few short years.

Most people experiencing such sudden tragedies, taking on the dimensions of those which engulfed the author's life, would most likely feel a quick crumbling of their heart, mind and inner spirit. . .but not Evelyn.

Evelyn Taylor-McNamara has turned painful adversity and cruel mental suffering into an instrument for the greater glory of our Lord Jesus Christ. She has given Him the total acknowledgement for the inner courage, strength, perseverance, and healing she has needed to weather her storms and find peace through a deeper relationship with Him.

It is Evelyn's stalwart conviction of bringing something wonderful and positive out of her personal tribulation and devastations, by recognizing how God would be using her in a mighty way, and in a mighty way He has.

In your daily walk with Him, let this special book be a new and useful tool in your arsenal for doing God's Will.

So pleased to have written this publishing endorsement.

Dahk Knox, Ph.D., Ed.D., Psy.D.
CEO/Publisher
The Tennessee Publishing House
Mosheim, Tennessee
July 2009

Prologue

My life changed the morning of December 23rd, as my precious husband, Kenneth, hurried off to deliver gifts to his valued clients. As the door closed, I had no idea that this would be the last time I would hear the familiar words: "I love you sweetheart. See you later."

With a multitude of activities cluttering my day, it was very difficult to hear the still, small voice of God. Christmas was only hours away and a lot of preparation had to be done. However, my heart was unusually heavy all day. I sang songs with Zack, our four-year old son, and wrapped gifts, but I could not shake the uneasiness in my chest.

As the hours ticked by, I realized that Kenneth was late and had not attempted to call. I knew something was wrong, so I began to pray and surrender to God in my moment of despair.

Just like King David, after hitting rock bottom, "…strengthed himself in the Lord." *1 Samuel 30:6 (KJV)* He resolved to trust God rather than give in to the despair that threatened to overwhelm him.

I, like King David, was facing a challenge that was far too great to handle. I realized God's promise in *Psalm 34:17 (KJV)* "The righteous cry and the Lord heareth, and delivereth them out of their troubles." I desperately needed strength to face the days ahead.

We gain clarity and direction when we voluntarily separate ourselves from the clamor of life, to sit in God's presence, and quietly pray.

Scriptures reveal a few powerful glimpses of Jesus' examples of prayerful solitude:

♦ *"...He went out into a mountain to pray, and continued all night in prayer to God." **Luke 6:12 (KJV)***

♦ In the transfiguration account, *"...He took Peter and John and James, and went up into the mountain to pray." **Luke 9:28 (KJV)***

♦ In the Garden of Gethsemane, ***Matthew 26:36-46 (KJV),*** Christ won his battle in a place of prayer. That night, when He got up off His knees in the Garden, He had direction, hope, and the strength necessary to endure Calvary for our sake.

I did not know what was happening, but I knew in my heart that I could trust the Father; spending time in prayer gave me what I needed for all that lay ahead.

This book has been written for people who may have experienced tragedy in their lives and so desperately need assurances of protection, peace, and help during troubled times. He wants to strengthen you so you can bear up under the weight of tough circumstances.

When you yield to God, at some point, you will probably look back and mark that day as the beginning of new growth in your faith. One of the promises that I hold dear is: *"My grace is sufficient for thee: for my strength is made perfect in weakness." **I Corinthians 12:9 (KJV)***

Two years after learning of Kenneth's murder, my son Zack, was kidnapped by armed men. After another soul wrenching night, I was reminded of how my "Heavenly Father" had been dependable, faithful, and present during the death of Zack's father.

Every promise that Jesus had made was perfectly fulfilled. I, once again, came to God, completely helpless, with a desire to love and obey Him. Jesus said, *"The one who comes to me I will certainly not cast out." **John 6:37 (KJV)*** For all eternity, God's love and passion has been fixed on us.

God was present that night with Zack. After his return home, my son revealed to me that he had prayed to his guardian angel to protect him. It touched me deeply to hear Zack tell his story. Imagine, at the tender age of six, he had turned to his Heavenly Father to deliver him from his enemies. ***Psalms 37:40 (KJV)***

Every good thing we have is ours through the cross of Christ and is validated by His resurrection. The resurrection is evidence that, no matter what happens, Jesus is able to lead us to victory in all circumstances.

God does not always choose to answer our prayers the way we want. Our comfort is not His greatest desire. What he wants more than anything is His glory. He is the only one who knows what circumstances will best bring about our genuine worship. We are generously blessed as we live the words of John the Baptist about Jesus: *"He must increase, but I must decrease." **John 3:30 (KJV)***

Chapter 1

As the late night hours crept by, one endless second at a time, I held a picture of little Zack. His enormous brown eyes seemed to be looking straight back at me. I wondered, "Is he cold, or hungry, scared...or dead?"

Around me the house bustled with tense activity, as FBI agents connected a separate phone line they could use so mine wouldn't be tied up if the kidnappers called. My pastor made coffee. Family and friends were carrying on conversations, speculating...while my life had stopped.

An FBI agent spoke above the commotion. "It's urgent that you get your cars out from around this place so it'll have a normal appearance just in case the kidnappers are watching. Most of you will have to go now."

Another agent seated himself opposite me. "Mrs. Taylor, there will be a call from whoever took Zack, sooner or later. You will answer the phone, and remember this – be calm. Agree with everything they want, no matter what it is, and listen for identifiable background sounds. Keep talking...stall, stall, stall!"

Suddenly, I caught a glimpse of my parents coming up the walk. I ran out to them wanting to be the one to break the news. My mother had a severe asthma condition, and stress could aggravate it.

"So what's happened here?" my father said cheerfully when he saw I was okay. "I could tell something was wrong when you called a little while ago. Then when one of your neighbors came over and told us your burglar alarm had gone off, we decided to come and check on you. Is everything all right?"

"Daddy, they took your car." I answered, delaying the worst news until I could get Mom inside.

"Oh, so that's why you wanted the tag number!" he chuckled in relief. "Don't worry, it's only a car, and it's insured. I'm just glad y'all are okay!"

The words pierced my heart like a nail.

"Where's Zack?" Mom asked as she settled at the kitchen table. "I bet he's starved to death."

"Mom...they...they took Zack."

"Oh, no! Not my baby!" she screamed, then began to gasp for air. "Why didn't...you...tell us?"

"I thought...hoped to get him back before I..." my voice broke.

"I'll go home and get your pills, Jessie." Daddy's white face worried me as he rushed out.

"Tell...me…" mom insisted, trying to compose herself.

"I'd like to get your account, too." A new FBI agent had just arrived. "My name is Marta Jenkins." She flashed her identification and slid in beside me at the table. "I know you've already been questioned by the other agents, but I'd like to hear it first hand. Tell me what happened from the beginning, Mrs. Taylor." She began writing something on a note pad.

I took a deep breath and began the story. "Burt had brought a deposit from Knoxville and came to check on me after the accident." My words were tumbling out incoherently. I prayed for calm, for order in my thoughts.

"Burt Artis is your business partner, right?" the agent interrupted, shuffling papers and referring to her notes.

"That's right. Kenneth, my late husband, had a good head for figures, so he managed our vending business. Mr. Artis handled the mechanical part. After Kenneth was killed, Burt and I remained partners. He handled the Knoxville area while my father took care of the Newport end."

"Tell me about your accident." The agent said.

"A few days ago, I was in a car wreck and broke my hand. I had borrowed my Dad's car while mine was being fixed. Burt was worried and came to check on Zack and me. He not only is a business partner, but a close friend."

"Are you in the habit of locking your doors at night?"

"Always."

"How do you explain the kidnappers getting in without breaking or tampering with the lock?"

"I can't."

"Go on, Mrs. Taylor," the agent instructed, "what happened tonight?"

"Like I said, Burt was here. It was about 8:30 and I had just put Zack in his Winnie-the-Pooh pajamas. We were playing with him in his bedroom before he went to sleep. Suddenly, I heard a noise and turned around. Two men were standing in the doorway. The stocking masks over their heads caused their faces to look disfigured. The biggest man had a sawed-off shotgun, the smaller one, a pistol."

"Git down on the floor! one gunman growled."

"Burt and I obeyed without question or struggle, but Zack screamed in terror as they put duct tape around our hands."

"Don't do that to me!" he shrieked.

"Please, don't hurt us, I pleaded. They ignored me and began to search the house."

"Just take what you came after and get out of here!" Burt snapped.

"Shut up or I'll blow your head off!" one of them yelled.

"Where are the car keys?" the smaller man shouted at me.

"Hanging in the kitchen on a hook." I answered, thinking they would take the car and leave, but after they got the keys, they came back down the hall and went into my bedroom. They must have mistaken my burglar alarm for the light, because they accidentally set it off, then panicked and started cursing at us.

"Get what you came for and go!" Burt repeated so harshly, I was afraid they would kill us to shut him up!

Instead, the biggest man came back into the room and grabbed Zack up like a sack of potatoes! I'll never forget that scene. As they bolted down the hall, lamps and pictures toppled from Zack's frantic kicks. His terrified screams broke my heart. Somehow, I twisted and tore the duck tape from my wrists. There had to be unseen Hands helping me. I ran down the hall as they were getting into the car.

"Stop! Come back here, Evelyn. Untie me!" Burt screamed, but I kept going.

They had stuffed Zack between them in the front seat but the car door was still open. In spite of the guns, I lunged for him. With a violent shove, the burly man knocked me into the carport's brick wall. I fell, legs under the car. As they whirled out of the driveway the front wheels had to have rolled over me but I never felt the weight of this two-ton vehicle! Only a miracle from God saved me from being crushed. Barefooted, I ran after them. The car disappeared, leaving behind only the wisps of fog from the tail pipe, and the horrible, chilling sound of Zack's screams echoing in the cold night air.

Every panting breath I drew as I raced back to the house was a prayer for Zack. I frantically tried to call out but the phone was dead.

"Untie me!" yelled Burt. "Don't call the police, that'll just get him killed!"

However, I had only one goal in mind and hardly heard Burt as I ran around to see what had happened to the phone. "The extension in the office was off the hook and I replaced it. After I finally got dial-tone, I called Dad for the license plate number of your car. I wanted to give it to the police."

"And your Dad didn't know it," Mom said, slowly shaking her head. "Now it all makes sense. Neither of us could figure out why you needed to call when you could have gone out to get the number for yourself, or what you wanted it for."

"Go on Mrs. Taylor," the agent said. "What did you do then?"

"I called the police, then untied Burt."

"Here are your pills, Jessie," Daddy said to Mom as he came back in. "Come on, why don't you lie down on Evelyn's bed and rest for a while."

"I'm sorry," the agent said. "You and your wife will both have to go home. We need as few cars and distractions as possible. I'll let you know as soon as we hear anything. I promise."

After that, the agent proceeded with other business.

I began to pace from room to room to release the tension.

In Zack's room, the duct tape was still lying on the floor. That earlier scene flashed in my head: Me, 5 feet tall, 100 pounds, with a broken hand, easily breaking the tape, but this big husky man, had to lie helpless until I set him free. Strange. I started to pick up the mess.

"Don't do that, Mrs. Taylor!" the agent's voice startled me. "Leave everything just as it is. We haven't finished dusting for finger-prints."

Zack's bed was turned down, waiting for him, his clothes laid out for tomorrow. The room echoed with emptiness. My gaze rested on some rough places at the bottom of his bookshelf where, just a few weeks earlier, he had chipped the wood with his new Tonka truck.

"Now Zack," I had scolded, "you need to be more careful with your toys."

I would give anything for him to be there right now, busily chipping away.

My thoughts drifted back six years, to the first time I held Zack.

"I'm sorry Mrs. Taylor." the doctor's words rang in my ears. "Your high blood pressure and recent toxemia has forced me to recommend that you never have any-more children." But the sight of such a beautiful bundle had softened that blow…until now!

I walked back to the living room. My once cozy lit-tle home was not mine anymore…at least not for now. I couldn't touch or move anything. Agents were using a magnifying glass and tweezers to pick through my carpet, dust was covering everything as they tried to retrieve prints.

Muffled voices drifted out behind the closed office door. The agents were questioning Burt. "I guess they're just doing their job." I thought, but it was a waste of valu-able time. Burt didn't know any more than I did.

The Valentines Zack had been signing that evening were still on the coffee table. He was so proud of his newly acquired writing skill. I had helped him with the addresses.

Zack had been so excited about his first grade party tomorrow…or was it today already? I glanced at the clock expecting hours to have passed. Instead, the hands had crept forward only a few minutes.

My gaze settled back on the brightly colored envelopes when suddenly I caught a glimpse of one that I hadn't seen earlier. The letter "**M**" just barely showed from beneath the pile. I reached out, hands trembling, and slowly pulled it from among the others. "Who…" then I saw "**MOM**" so carefully written in Zack's small hand.

I stifled a sob. "Lord, give me a sign that he's okay." Since I couldn't cover Zack in person, I wrapped him in a prayer. I asked God to protect my son with the shield of his love while I imagined him surrounded by clear crystal, much like a delicate, rare flower secured under glass.

I tried to push fear away, but how could I when only recently…the very worst had happened… "Lord, You offer so many promises. I accept them, for Zack, for us."

The phone rang, jarring my reverie, snapping the agents to their stations.

Chapter 2

"Hello." I answered, attempting to master a tremor.

A brusque voice came over the line. "We got your boy, lady. Now you git us $200,000.00 by noon tomorrow."

"Is Zack okay?" I pleaded.

"Jus' git the money." The ugly voice demanded.

A click and a dial-tone made my knees weak. It brought back the sickening feeling in the pit of my stomach, which I had known earlier that evening when I had turned, and found myself staring down the barrel of a sawed-off shotgun.

In the flurry of activity, an agent accidentally brushed a plaque I had on the wall and knocked it down.

"I'm sorry, Mrs. Taylor." He picked it up and handed it to me. My eyes rested on the words. I had written this poem and prayer when I found out I was pregnant with Zack.

"OUR BABY"

9-17-73

(Dedicated to our precious Baby
on this 2nd month of his creation)

B   *is for the **BLESSING** of which **GOD** will entrust to us the day you come into our lives-*

A   *is for the **ADMIRATION** we will have for you because you are our very own buddle of love-*

B   *is for **BEING** just you and for the innocence and sweetness you will possess-*

Y   *is for the future **YEARS** we trust will be ours for the asking; uniting us closely as a family of love and respect for each other and our Heavenly Father, forgetting not that he is our "Creator".*

PRAYER: *Oh, God, on this the 17th day of September, I dedicate our little one to You and ask that You would take his little life and lead him through all his battles, victories, disappointments, and failures, giving him strength and faith to face each new day with a deep understanding of You. Help Kenneth and I, as parents, bring him up according to Your plan and bless us by entering into his* *tender little heart, giving him a home in heaven, as You have promised in your written Word. Thus, we will never have to part as Mother, Daddy, and Child. Unite us together as a family, I pray. Amen.*

With all my love,
Mom

Little did I know when I wrote the prayer six years ago, how much it would mean to me at this moment!

"What if Zack didn't come back? What if…" I tried not to think of the time two years earlier when, like now, I waited for someone I loved, and what had occurred then. I was exhausted, yet unable to sleep. "What is happening to my baby…so small, defenseless, and trusting?"

My prayers covered him until there was little else to pray.

Burt and the agent came out of the office. I smiled at him, trying to be reassuring. He looked so nervous, clenching and releasing his fists, eyes darting at the clock. Occasionally he glanced at me, but never came over to talk.

As hours crawled on, the present began to merge with the past until, in spite of my willing it away, I lived again another dark night of waiting, of struggling to hope.

On that occasion, the night before Christmas Eve, 1978, Zack was four. It would be the first Christmas to really remember. Our little family had always looked forward to the holidays. It meant my hard working husband would be home.

Kenneth was an ambitious salesman in a demanding career, which often kept him out until ten or eleven at night. His route sometimes took him to secluded, remote areas and I worried about his carrying large sums of money.

We owned a vending business. The machines were placed in various markets and Kenneth would restock the inventory and collect the money. He was a cracker-jack businessman, but I felt he was naïve when it came to judging people's character.

Sometimes he would help a new business get off the ground by fronting the money or extending credit. Many times people would take advantage of his generosity, but he always said, "God takes care of His own," and with unshakable faith, he ventured into these out-of-the-way places.

"I'll be home early tomorrow night. There are just a few customers I haven't seen yet this week. I want to get their Christmas gifts to them before I take off for the holidays. You both be dressed up. We'll go out to dinner."

Kenneth winked and smiled. He loved to surprise us with little treats.

I laid out his green suit and cowboy boots to save time the next morning. "The quicker he gets started, the earlier he'll be home," I reasoned. We went to sleep that night, peacefully expecting a tomorrow that seemed so certain.

Evelyn and Zack

Chapter 3

When I awakened, I reached across to find Kenneth's side empty. Pulling open the draperies, I saw the sun shining on the low-hanging clouds, high-lighting their lines with gold and rose. They reminded me of gigantic fluffy pillows.

In spite of such beauty an ominous sense of fore-boding settled over me. Trying to escape the feeling, I immersed myself in housework, tidying areas already shining. The uneasiness persisted.

Christmas is a happy time. Ever since I accepted Jesus when I was eighteen, this time of year had brought an even greater awareness of intimacy with the Lord. Christ had come to save me, to give me a new kind of life. I could feel and experience His loving Spirit. My own spirit responded to Him, and to His gifts.

In every direction, designs of nature, laughter with friends, caresses of Kenneth and Zack's tender hugs, all this had been planned for me by a heavenly Father. Still, none of these replaced or supplanted Christ's love. Jesus just made everything more precious! Why then, did I feel this apprehension, this nameless dread?

As 5:00PM neared, Zack and I decided to make a game out of getting ready. Each of us bathed, and then selected our very best outfits.

"I beat ya, Mommy!" he squealed excitedly as he rounded the corner to my room. The dangling shoelaces that he couldn't tie yet tangled under his feet and he fell face down on the soft carpet. We both burst into giggles.

"So you did!" I praised his achievement then lifted him to the bed to tie his shoes.

As I kneeled in front of him, busy with the laces, he watched me intently.

"You are so pretty, Mommy." He brushed the hair back from my face. "Wait 'till Daddy sees!"

I hugged this special little boy, but the knot in my stomach was relentless.

The Christmas tree brightly glimmered over the enticing packages. Cookie fragrances tantalized, but we would wait to eat them. Scented candles burned lower as we waited for the familiar sound of Kenneth's truck in the drive.

Zack gently fingered the porcelain nativity scene on the end table. "Tell me again, Mommy." He whispered in reverence. His eyes were riveted to the figures.

I told Zack the story of the Bible at Bethlehem, of the Wisemen who had waited, and followed the Star for so very long, the shepherds, the angels, and Mary and Joseph, all of them waiting for the promise of Jesus.

For Zack, the story was fresh and new, filled with wonder.

"Baby Jesus had gifts, too." He pointed.

Each gift had special meaning, though Zack was too young to understand what the Wiseman's gifts meant, then.

"You know, Daddy had presents to deliver today. Surprises for our friends, and his customers."

I patted the cushion beside me. Happily, he bounded to the couch. As we waited, Zack's gaze strayed from window to tree and back until finally he slid to the floor and sat as near to the presents as possible.

I had always decorated two trees: a formal one for Kenneth in the living room and a traditional one for Zack in the den. Ours was covered with tiny white twinkle lights and gold trimmings. Underneath were Kenneth's presents, wrapped in gold paper and ribbons.

Zack's tree was covered with Hallmark collectables and handmade ornaments. His presents were brightly colored shapes and sizes, ever beckoning this four-year-old miniature whirlwind of activity. In his quiet moments, he could usually be found shaking and rearranging his packages, hardly able to contain his excitement in the endless wait before Christmas morning.

"When we gonna eat, Mommy?"

Although the mantle clock over the fireplace showed only 5:45PM, that uneasy feeling intensified. Inwardly, I agonized, "What is wrong? All Kenneth was doing today was delivering gifts to the customers in Knoxville and Morristown. This night is as important to him as to us. Could he be having car trouble?"

Zack sighed, still waiting for an answer. "Soon, honey. Daddy will be here soon, and then we'll go eat."

I went to the kitchen, poured a cup of hot coffee and settled myself at the table where I could see the clock, and also through the living room window to the driveway. Steam drifted slowly from my cup and the clock ticked, playing a macabre accompaniment for the silent rhythm of the twinkle lights.

Suddenly Zack jumped up, remembering some-thing, and ran excitedly to his room.

"Mommy!" he appeared again in the doorway with two little presents. "I 'most forgot! These are for you and Daddy. Let's put 'em under the tree!" His big brown eyes danced with all the mischief of a preschooler trying to keep a secret.

Zack's kindergarten teacher had helped the class with their presents. The gift wrap was his creation: white paper colored with acrylic paint and tied with a piece of red knitting yarn. These were the first gifts Zack had ever given.

We went to place the packages beneath Kenneth's tree with the appropriate fanfare for bestowal of a king's treasure. There, nestled in all the gold presents, Zack proudly perceived them as precious gems, gleaming in an otherwise ordinary setting.

I returned to the couch, and waited. Seven, eight o'clock, no Kenneth. Christmas music droned from the stereo. Somehow this usually pleasurable tradition began to get to my nerves.

Zack silently twisted the limbs of his G.I. Joe, plac-ing him in various attack positions among the flower arrangement, magazines, and candy dish on the coffee table, at the same time keeping a careful eye on me. His movements were beginning to reflect my tension.

"Zack," I said as cheerfully as I could muster. "I'm going to fix a sandwich for you. It's too late to go out to eat now, but I promise we'll go tomorrow night."

He ate silently. After tucking him in bed, I returned to the living room.

Nine o'clock, 10:00PM, 11:00PM, 12:00AM. My panic was so intense; it threatened to drag me into hysteria. Finally, I laid down on our bed, fully dressed, eyes wide open and stared into the room, waiting, listening. "Should I call someone? But who?" The closest relative was 50 miles away and it was late. I hated to bother them, especially if it turned out to be something simple...like a flat tire.

I tried to think pleasant things. My mind wandered back through the years, selecting happy memories as one would pick the loveliest flowers from a garden array.

Kenneth and I met when I was a high school senior. He was eight years older than I, and my father wouldn't allow me to date. I thought he was the most handsome man I'd ever known and was extremely flattered he even noticed me. No matter how much I pleaded, Daddy stood firm.

Kenneth was undaunted, however, and continued to lay a foundation of trust and friendship with Daddy. He proved to be an excellent salesman: his most notable sale being the one of himself to my Dad! After I graduated, Daddy allowed me to follow my heart.

Kenneth saw the Lord's hand in our relationship. I was eighteen years old and not sure of God's plan for my life at that time. As we got to know each other, I saw what a wonderful loving spirit he had and the commitment he had to our Saviour. There was no doubt in his mind that God had put him in my life so we could serve Him more completely as one. Four years later, we were married.

The mantle clock struck 3:00AM. The house was so quiet, my stomach was doing flip-flops. I felt a desperate need to hear some gospel music, so I reached for a tape on the bedside table.

A few weeks earlier I had found the song For *Those Tears I Died* and it quickly became a favorite of Kenneth's and mine. I had recorded it and he had nearly worn out the tape. As I placed it in the player, a distant memory flooded my head.

"You could really be a big star, a millionaire." The agent tempted me with fame and fortune. This was exciting to hear and impressive to a girl of eighteen. I was flattered.

The contract in country music would be a dream come true, but my new relationship with Jesus somehow caused me to have an uneasy feeling about this offer.

"All I can think of is singing." I silently prayed to the Lord. "Tell me what you want."

The answer came in my next thought: "I want you to sing for Me." Much to this man's surprise and dismay, I turned down his offer. "This is the chance of a lifetime, Evelyn," he pleaded. "I know the Lord has something else out there for me. I have to follow His direction."

He went away, shaking his head at this "foolish" girl, but the peace in my heart assured me I had done the right thing.

My gaze fell on the coat I had laid out for our missed evening excursion, and a Christmas Eve memory flashed into my head.

From the moment we met, Kenneth and I seemed so close we could sometime communicate without saying a word—as happened on this occasion.

We had been married only a year or so, and as most young couples just starting out, our funds were limited. We left our small apartment that night to go to K-Mart for some last minute Christmas shopping.

The weather was unseasonably cold, and Kenneth and I shrank deep into our coats as we hurried across the parking lot. A slender, little woman by the front door caught our attention. She was holding a cup for donations and shivering in her thin cotton print dress and patched sweater.

"Where do you live?" Kenneth asked striking up a conversation. He had an enthusiastic personality and a way of loving everyone he met.

"Behind Sears, on Central Avenue" she replied. "My husband was hurt and unable to work. I'm trying to get enough money to buy a present for each of my two children before the store closes." She seemed embarrassed and ill at ease. I felt this was a decent, hard working family that had truly fallen on hard times.

"Why aren't you wearing a coat?" I asked. "It's too cold to be out here without one."

She hung her head and murmured, "I don't have one."

During the time we were in the store, this pitiful woman weighed on our mind. When we got back to the car, Kenneth and I looked at each other.

"Are you thinking what I'm thinking?" I asked.

He nodded and I saw that old familiar twinkle in his eye when he was excited about something.

We rushed home, and Kenneth went to the kitchen while I went to my closet. I only had two coats, the one I was wearing, and nicer one I kept to wear to church. I took the better one from the closet and put it in a bag, then went to help Kenneth.

We happily worked together, packing grocery sacks with the special food planned for our own Christmas dinner, then hurried back to K-Mart. By the time we got there, though, the store was closed and the woman gone. For a minute, we sat silently in disappointment, then…

"Central Avenue!" Kenneth announced. "She said she lived behind Sears."

"But there must be 25 or 30 homes back there." I muttered.

Not about to be dissuaded, Kenneth proceeded to Central Avenue. We drove up and down the street looking at the poor, run-down homes before Kenneth suddenly stopped at one of them.

I remained in the car while he went to the front door. In just a minute, he waived for me to join him. What a grin he had on his face! Amazingly, out of all the houses in the area, we had parked in front of the very one belonging to the family we were seeking!

The children squealed while happy tears trembled on the woman's cheeks as we unloaded the bags.

This was one of the best Christmases Kenneth and I ever had! A chilling wind whipped against the windows of the tiny house, but the glow of true Christmas spirit warmed the hearts of us all.

I glanced at the clock. Four-thirty in the morning. Outside, enormous black clouds rolled over the stars and hid them from my view.

A storm was on the way. From the safety of my bed, I felt strangely part of it—the eerie darkness, the pelting rain, thunder rumbling like a rock slide. Inside, I felt the same sense of turbulence.

I told myself every possible explanation for Kenneth's tardiness, but, still, the dread turned into a fear that overwhelmed all the logic in the world. I was suddenly reminded of the promise, given in *Proverbs 3:25 (KJV)*, *"Be not afraid of sudden fear, neither of the desolation of the wicked, when it cometh."* because the Lord shall be our confidence.

Kenneth and Evelyn

Chapter 4

The first rays of morning sun peeked through the vanishing clouds. I stared outside at the empty driveway, as if willing it to put Kenneth's truck where it belonged. My eyes drifted to the huge Oak, spreading its almost barren branches over the frost-burnt lawn. Drops of rain were glistening from the few remaining leaves stubbornly clinging to life—essentially laughing in the face of their appointed passing.

As long as I had known Kenneth, he had always kept appointments. He was a responsible man who loved his family and wouldn't intentionally worry us—especially on Christmas Eve!

"Did you admit a Kenneth Taylor last night? He is about 5' 11", dark curly hair, brown eyes, forty years old." I repeated this to each area hospital. None had seen anyone by that name or description. At last, I decided to get a babysitter for Zack and search on my own.

Traffic was light. As I passed residential areas, I could visualize families preparing their Christmas dinners, wrapping last minute packages, and stoking fire logs. I felt a pang of jealousy. "We should be doing those things!" I thought. "Here I am driving around, frantically trying to find my missing husband!"

One family was loading the car with gifts and suit-cases for an obvious reunion. The children's faces were bursting with excitement; one teased her mother with a present. I heard the echoes of *Joy to the World* sung a bit off-key, but with great gusto. Could anyone see my con-cern, feel my panic? Did anyone look at all? The world went on as usual, unaware of my anxiety.

I spent most of the day searching, hurling prayer after prayer toward heaven. None of Kenneth's customers had seen him. I stopped frequently to call home, but the babysitter had not heard anything either.

Turning the car around, I headed toward the rural areas of Kentucky where Kenneth serviced some country stores.

"Maybe he decided to check on one of his cus-tomers up here." I hoped.

Civilization seemed to disappear. Mountains, trees, and steep cliffs took its place. Low hanging branches closed in on me as I pulled onto a narrow road. "I think this is the way...or is it?"

A late afternoon winter chill went straight through me. The car was becoming bound by the fog so prevalent in the mountains this time of year. My knuckles were white against the steering wheel; my forearms ached from the tension.

I drove slowly, examining the guard rails and underbrush along the road for signs of recent breakage. The cliffs were so steep, I couldn't see the bottom. One particularly sharp curve had a small shoulder, so I stopped and got out. Stepping to the edge, I searched the incline until I became dizzy. I closed my eyes and breathed deeply of the cold, clean pine-scented air and listened to the stillness.

Suddenly, a shudder jarred my body as I heard the blood-chilling howls of a distant dog pack. Quickly, I got back in the car and turned toward home.

"Maybe Kenneth's truck will be there when I get back." I tried positive thoughts.

Rounding the corner to my street, I saw a vehicle was in the drive, but it was my brother Matt's car, not Kenneth's.

When I opened the front door, I spotted my pastor sitting on the fireplace hearth. He and Matt forced a smile as I came in, but their faces told a different story.

"I can't find Kenneth. I've been out looking for him and I can't......" I shook my head, trying to delay the inevitable by talking, but I was too exhausted to continue.

"Evelyn, sit down." Reverend Keener said.

"He's dead isn't he?" I asked.

"Don't get upset." he continued. "They've found a body on the Blue Ridge Parkway. He had on a green suit and cowboy boots..." his voice trailed off.

At first, I felt almost a sense of relief. At least I knew something definite. Then fear, anger, and despair surged over me. Matt was saying something, but his words only made a discordant background for the thoughts swirling in my head: "Why are You letting this happen to us, God? Kenneth has been a good man, husband, and father. I am a faithful wife and mother. Why this?"

"Honey," Matt's words cut through the confusion, "go pack a suitcase and come back to Newport with me."

I walked dry-eyed into my bedroom. It was almost as if another, stronger person was taking over.

The poem called *Footprints* tells of two sets of footprints in the sand signifying the poet's walk with God.

The last paragraph states when times are roughest, there is only one set visible.

The poet asks, "Why did you leave me during those times?" and the Lord answered, "It was during those times that I carried you."

It wasn't until later that I became aware of the reality of this. I had retreated into a new place. A place I had never been before. A place we go to when we can't feel anymore. When things happen that are so devastating we can't even pray, or think, the great Comforter takes over. It was during this time that Jesus carried me.

Zack - Age 4

Chapter 5

Christmas day arrived, torn open like a package. Some of the family went back to the house in Knoxville and got Zack's gifts. I sat on my brother Allen's couch, alone on an island of despair, oblivious to happenings around me.

One thing that penetrated was the twinkle lights on Allen's Christmas tree, marking each agonizing second, a continuation of two nights earlier. As I stared at the lights, each flash seared that bitter, sickening association into my consciousness.

The following days were a blur. FBI agents bombarded me with questions about Kenneth. Relatives were coming and going around a swirl of activity. "What suit do you want him buried in?" "Do you know who might want to hurt Kenneth?" "What flowers do you want on the casket?" "Was there a business partner or customer with an ax to grind?" "What do I tell Kenneth's customers, the press?" Their questions began to meld together.

The morning of the funeral, Mom came in the bedroom as I was getting ready. "What do you want Zack to wear?"

"I…I think he's too young to go. He won't understand especially if he sees his Daddy in the casket. Please…do you know someone reliable to stay with him?"

"Don't worry, I'll handle it." she said as she put her arms around my shoulders.

"That's a pretty dress, Mom. Have I seen it before?" I asked in an attempt at small talk.

"I got it for Christmas." Her voice broke slightly. "I didn't expect this to be the first…"

"Mom," I interrupted her before the tears came, "would you put this outfit on Zack?"

She took the little shirt and pants I had picked from the suitcase. "It's amazing." Mom began as she looked at the neatly folded clothes. "You packed exactly enough to get through this week. I don't know if I would have been able to think ahead like that."

"I didn't, Mom…God did. I don't remember putting one thing in this case."

As I walked into the funeral home, the director greeted me. Paul gently took me by the arm and led me to the family's waiting room.

"I know…usually…you would be familiar with the procedure, Evelyn…" he began.

"Paul, as many times as I've been here to sing, I've never……I've…I…"

Paul compassionately patted my hand as he explained the order of service. "Do you have any special requests?"

"There's a song…*For Those Tears I Died*. Kenneth loved it so much. Someone's gone to the house to get it."

"Anything else?"

"Yes, I want to see him."

As Paul and I entered the Chapel, I glanced around the room. The soon to be filled chairs, the low lights and soft curtains, were all encased in unnatural stillness. The sweet fragrance from the flowers was almost sickening.

"Please, open it."

"Evelyn…" Paul looked uncomfortable. "I can't"

"But I want to touch him, to see him one last time."

"No, you can't."

I stared at the casket, too weak to argue anymore. The flowers in the center were beautiful…roses…red and white, so perfect for Christmas. Christmas! My mind struggled back to reality. The last time I had seen Kenneth, he was laughing and happy, excited about the holidays. I just wanted to tell him once more how much I loved him. There was so much left to say and this unexpected death left me feeling cheated.

The outside doors jerked open, startling me. I turned around to see Kenneth's family enter. How fragile his mother looked. Instantly, my heart went out to them. This was the second tragic loss in the family. A few years earlier, Kenneth's eighteen-year old brother had been shot and killed.

Friends began to come in and I knew I needed to take my position to greet them, but I just couldn't tear myself away from the casket. As I rubbed the smooth copper top, suddenly my hand brushed one of the roses. Some of the petals fell, and in my state of mind I felt as if I had "hurt" it somehow. My heart jumped to my throat, my breath was coming in short gasps. My only thought was, "I need to be strong for Kenneth's family." I rushed out to try and compose myself.

In the hall, I looked for a quiet place, but there were people everywhere. Their sympathetic stares and expressions of condolence bounced off the shield of numbness that covered me.

My knees nearly buckled under me as I pushed open the door to the lady's room. The queasiness in my stomach threatened to make me violently ill. Drops of sweat ran down my neck, the room began to sway. I steadied myself against the cold porcelain sink.

"Dear God, help me get through this." I cried.

Suddenly, the words, *"My flesh and my heart fail, but God is the strength of my heart, and a portion forever!"* echoed against the tile walls.

I whirled around, eyes probing the empty room.

"...God is the strength of my heart...."

The soothing words washed over me as a cool shower on a blistering summer day. Then I realized, God was with me...as close as if He was standing right there beside me! That comforting scripture, tucked back in the deep recesses of my memory, had come bubbling forth as a fountain just when I needed it most. God's Words were real and personal to me, an anchor in the most devastating storm.

I felt my anguish and frustrations disappear like so many shadows in the sunshine. "I don't understand this, Lord, but I know You are here. You are the strength of my heart."

Chapter 6

Over the next few days, when I needed most to withdraw, to rest, everything overwhelmed me. There were so many things to deal with, so many bills, so many decisions. A "responsibility storm" battered my spirit until it was bent.

"I don't have the strength for this Lord." I prayed, feeling the words come from a place so deep inside, it seemed to have no bottom.

I had noticed how unsettled Zack was. He couldn't understand why we were in a strange place, his home gone, his father missing, his confidence shaken. "Dear God, I need You! I accept the difficulty life has handed me, but please show me how to cope with it…and how to tell Zack."

I thumbed through the worn, dog-eared pages of the Bible Kenneth had given me. *"Call upon Me in the day of trouble: I will deliver thee…"* **Psalms 50:15 (KJV)** jumped out at me, cutting through the mists of pain. I seized this scripture like a drowning person clutches a rope.

Zack was playing by the couch. I joined him on the floor.

"Honey, I have something to talk to you about. It's kind of hard for me, but Jesus is going to help."

Zack looked up in anticipation, sensing the importance of my words.

"I know you have been wondering why we are staying with Uncle Allen instead of our house, and why your Daddy's not here."

He nodded.

"Zack, your Daddy is dead. He's okay, though, because he's in heaven."

Zack looked at me with a question in his eyes. I knew he was too young to understand death...does anyone? Then God brought something to my memory.

"Do you remember the first time you went to day-care?"

Zack nodded silently. There was a tinge of pain on his face, confirming I was on the right track.

"You cried, and wanted to go home with me, didn't you?"

"Yeah."

"Mrs. Jacobs' house had a room where mothers could stay and not be seen. You didn't know this, but as soon as I left you in the mornings, I would go there and watch you. I was so close, I could have reached out and touched you, but you didn't know it."

Surprise covered Zack's little face, then a grin. "Like hide 'n seek!"

"Right!" I hugged him and silently thanked God for the words. Zack snuggled deep in my arms.

"God's heaven is like that Zack. He is so close to us, always watching, protecting, but we can't see him." The hint of a tear moistened my eyes. "Daddy has gone to heaven to live with God, but in his place, He has sent a guardian angel to watch over you."

I took the Bible from the coffee table and turned to **Matthew 18:10 (KJV).** *"Take heed that ye despise not one of these little ones; for I say unto you that in heaven their angels do always behold the face of my Father, who is in heaven."*

"What is…gar…garden?"

"Guardian means 'one who protects'. Jesus said your angel will keep you safe and watch over you."

"Can I see him?"

"No, just like God, your angel can be near without being seen. Let's pray and thank God for watching over us."

"Dear God," I began, "thank You for being there when we need You...."

"...and thank You for my 'garden angel'! Amen"

After that night, Zack was a different child. Every evening he would say his prayers and thank God for his **"garden angel"**.

On New Year's Eve, the church had a special watch night service. It was only one week after Kenneth's death and I didn't want to go. The ringing church bells brought a pang of fear and dread. "I don't know how to do this..." I prayed. "I don't know how to go back to just being me...without him. I've never felt so lonely. How can I go into the new year without Kenneth?"

About a week later a voice woke me in the night.

"Evelyn, Evelyn, help me!"

I jumped and my skin prickled as I felt a presence in the dark room. Turning over, I searched the shadows with bleary eyes. Suddenly, I recognized his familiar form in the doorway.

"Kenneth!" I gasped. At that moment, the clouds rolled back, allowing the dim moonlight to illuminate him, revealing a huge bunch of bright red roses in his hand. I started to reach for him, but when I did, a petal from one of the blooms fell. It floated to the carpet like an enormous snowflake on a windless winter night. Then, one at a time, all the other pedals drifted to the floor until the stems were bare.

I jerked awake, dripping in perspiration and shaking violently. I turned on the lamp, but the room was empty.

"Dear God, please relieve me of these dreams." I prayed desperately. "I'm turning it all over to You. Give me the strength to get through this."

The nightmares never returned. God took them away. The Bible promises: *"And all things, whatever ye shall ask in prayer, believing, ye shall receive." Matthew 21:22 (KJV)* I had always believed in God's promises, but there is nothing like seeing them in action to build one's faith.

Two weeks after I buried Kenneth, someone from my church died.

"Evelyn, I hate to ask," Jill said when she called me, "but could you sing at Dad's funeral? I know it would be hard, especially since…well, anyway, he loved to hear you sing…"

My mind was reeling. How could I do this? The funeral would be held in the same place as Kenneth's. However, I felt a strong assurance and peace from God, so I agreed.

The casket was in the exact spot where Kenneth's had been two weeks earlier. The usual position of the singer was directly behind the casket. I really prayed for God to give me the courage and calm to get through this. It was time to step forward. "Lord, I give my voice completely to You."

Many people commented later about the blessing they received that day, knowing the recent circumstances I had faced. God turned my song into a great public testimony for His grace and power and I praise Him for using me in that way.

That winter there was so much snow, almost as if God was trying to cover the earth's blackness and evil. I often got in my car and drove, even in icy conditions when no one else was on the road. Not caring that it was dangerous or not, I would go all the way to Knoxville and spend the day in the mall. Other times, I would walk in my neighborhood.

I felt a need for exercise to release tension, but little did I know the other benefits I would receive from this activity.

By the time I covered five or six blocks each day, I would begin to relax. Scriptures came to mind as I traveled and I would recite them. My favorite, *"Yet I will rejoice in the Lord, I will joy in the God of my salvation!"* **Habakkuk 3:1 (KJV))** Every time a sad thought would try to slip in, I would make it flee with this verse.

I also discovered this was an ideal time to talk to the Lord. I thanked God for my blessings, for Zack, my parents and family. All around there was so much to be thankful for: the spring flowers, and chirping birds, the summer rain, the fall leaves and crisp air, the winter snow and promise of a new beginning. My prayer life deepened, my depression eased.

I thought of Kenneth often…what we would have been doing now…and twenty years from now. We had been looking forward to retiring young, going places, doing things, but life had dealt us a cruel blow.

We had dreamed. All those dreams were dashed. Is there reason to dream again? I couldn't think of the future, yet, can one survive without it?

Every person has the choice of bringing joy, or hurt into their surroundings. Kenneth chose to bring joy, to leave happiness, to bless. His life represented Christ well. He made it his business to make a hole in the blackness of the world around him, letting in a ray of God's light so others could look beyond where there is no night.

"What does God have in store for me? How can He use me when I can't even feel anymore?"

God reads the thoughts of us all from moment to moment. I discovered He was reading mine.

While searching my Bible for answers one day, I heard the backdoor slam and the sound of Zack's wet rubber boots slapping across the kitchen floor.

"Mommy! Mommy!" he cried.

"What's the matter, Zack?" I ran to him.

"'urt self, Mommy 'urt self!" he sobbed as he showed me the torn pants knee.

Gently I peeled off the wet snow-crusted coat to get a better look. The warmth from the house began to "thaw out" his wound, causing the feeling to return and the blood to flow freely. The sight scared him and he started to cry hysterically.

"It 'urts, Mommy!" he wailed.

"Everything will be all right." I tried to calm his fears.

"Make it stop!"

"Honey, I can't take the hurt away. Only time can do that." I explained as I put the Band-Aid® over the scratch.

"Mommy," he said between sniffles as he wrapped his little arms around my neck, "will ya help me be bizzy 'till time works? …be bizzy 'till time works!"

Zack had complete faith in my ability to keep his mind off the hurt until it healed. I suddenly realized I am limiting God's love and power. He allows us to go through the hurt of this life to strengthen our faith and trust in Him, to let us know a new day will come.

I had been concentrating on sorrow, trying to heal myself. From the mouth of my small son, came under-standing: God doesn't want me to wait until I'm "healed" before He uses me! He wants me just as I am, broken and shattered. He wants to be the One who heals, who sup-plies, who sustains!

"Dear God," I prayed, "please help me 'be bizzy' in Your love and service until my hurt subsides."

Weeks passed. I was beginning to deal with grief fairly well until one day I was walking down the street in Newport and a total stranger came up to me.

"I'm sorry about Kenneth," she said, planting herself squarely in front of me. "They treated him like an animal, shooting his head off like they did and dumping him on the parkway. "That's so horrible!"

I was stunned. Until that moment, I had not known how it happened. I had never asked nor did I want to know. On the day of the funeral, it hadn't occurred to me why the casket remained closed. Somehow, I had been trying to deny it...make it gentler.

I went to the funeral home and got a copy of the death certificate. The section for the "cause of death" read: "Multiple gunshot wounds to the head."

That was the first time I had accepted what really happened, the first time I cried.

A good friend once told me, "Evelyn, you react to hurt like an oyster."

"An oyster?"

"When a piece of sand finds its way past the shell, sometimes it loges in the soft body tissue and becomes an irritation." She explained. "The oyster secretes a substance to cover it, trying to smooth out the rough edges, make it less painful." Ironically, the more the oyster tries to cover it up, the bigger it gets, becoming more painful as time goes by.

When we allow the Lord to work in our lives, He can take that hurt and, in His time, turn it into something wonderful—a 'pearl' of rare beauty; a jewel of wisdom.

Besides losing my beloved husband, there were so many kinds of hurts to face and, of course, I asked questions: of myself, of God, and of others. Had Jesus not cried at His crucifixion, *"My God, my God, why hast thou forsaken me?"* **Matthew 27:46 (KJV)**

It was not a sin to ask "why", but it could have become sin if I had entertained bitterness. I did ask, "Lord, why are some people so cruel?"

My question to God invited His answer and His help. He took charge, bringing a new kind of understanding. Until that moment, I had isolated myself in a world of memories, loneliness, and an attempt at denial of the reality of Kenneth's death. Healing comes from accepting what happens, then trusting God to use it for good and His glory.

I Understood all this in my head, but getting my heart to accept it was a different story.

Chapter 7

Over the next few weeks, I retreated inside myself, lost weight, was often sick, and fought depression. During one particular rough bout with the flu, my neighbor came over to bring me some soup and help Zack. "Come on," she insisted after seeing the shape I was in, "you are going to the doctor!"

Dr. Murray was a Christian. He worked out of St. Mary's Hospital in Knoxville. After the examination, he took me into his office.

"Have you been on a diet?" he asked.

"No." I replied, nervously fingering my purse. "A few weeks ago my husband was murdered. I've been having a hard time coping."

This extremely busy doctor could tell I was on edge and he took all the time necessary to hear my story. For the first time, someone made me talk about my feelings.I had been protecting my family and friends, not wanting to burden them, keeping it all inside. It was such a relief to finally release all my pent-up emotions. As I blurted out my story, tears ran down this kind man's face.

"Well, Evelyn," he said, "you've been a widow for five weeks. Kenneth has been gone long enough for you to realize just how great your loss really is."

"I feel so alone, so cheated."

"Because Kenneth was a Christian, you know he is in heaven, and because you believe that, you have to rethink your viewpoint of death as the ultimate tragedy. I think your grief is more for yourself than for Kenneth."

"I just don't have any answers to my questions." I said. "Why did it have to happen to Kenneth? To us? Why have they not solved this murder...?

"You are a child of God, and He has promised to supply your every need. He has also promised that you and Kenneth will both live forever with Him. Jesus came into this world to give us life. He is not the God of the tomb. But of resurrection morning!"

"I know what you are saying is true, Dr. Murray, but can you tell me how to really feel it inside?"

"Let's ask God to help."

I bowed my head with this man as he began to talk to God. "Lord, we don't understand Your ways, but we do know we want Your companionship and Your presence more than we want understanding." He reached over and took my hand. "So we choose You, Lord. It's up to You to decide when or if You want to give the answers. We believe in Your promises and claim them. Bring something beautiful out of this tragedy, we pray. In Jesus' precious Name we ask these things. Amen"

When he had finished, I felt drained, exhausted, but the unbearable, razor-edged sharpness of my pain was gone. God had begun the healing of my wounded spirit.

The Lord is sufficient for His children, but sometimes it helps to open up to another Christian. The support and advice this man gave helped speed the healing process.

Dr. Murray gave me a booklet entitled, *Comfort for Troubled Christians*, and a Vitamin B complex to help my anemia; however, it was his advice that helped the most. He wrote two Bible verses on the pad: ***Romans 8:18 (KJV):*** *"For I reckon that the sufferings of this present time are not worthy to be compared with the glory which shall be revealed in us,"* and ***Romans 8:28 (KJV):*** *"And we know that all things work together for good to them that love God, to them who are called according to his purpose."*

Dr. Charles Murray's understanding, compassion, and unique prescription were turning points in my recovery. I know the Lord led me to this man and made me thank God for His patience and direction.

In my grief, I could not fathom how having my husband horribly murdered could possibly bring any good at all. "All things work together for good...." All? *All*. It is God's Word. *"Forever, oh Lord, Your Word is settled in heaven."* **Psalm 119:89 (KJV)** But could the grossest possible evil turn to bring good?

In God's hands it can. So staggering, yet...I could not image this, nor could I grasp that never again there could be anything to delight me. I would discover that farther along any path in life God can bestow wonderful blessings. Now, looking back, I realize, God had been saving one for me!

I was to find peace and strength to cope with the harshness of life through His gift of singing. What I didn't know at that time was the extent to which He would use my voice as a witness for Him and a comfort to others in mourning.

One specific incident assured me that God was using my talent. A close friend had lost her father-in-law and had asked me to sing at his funeral. That week I had caught a bad cold which turned into laryngitis so severe,

I could barely whisper, and Sharon had asked me to sing Rise Again. I have an alto voice, and even under the best of circumstances, the high vocal range of the song was a stretch for me.

On the morning of the funeral, I called Sharon. "I can't sing today...." I whispered hoarsely into the phone.

"But Evelyn, you have to! It would mean so much to us!"

"Well, okay." I croaked. "With the help of the Lord, I'll try."

For the rest of the day, I gargled and sprayed my throat. By the time I arrived at the funeral home, I could not so much as whisper. "Lord, if this is Your will *You* will have to be my voice." I prayed. "But if this is not to be, give this family the peace and assurance of Your presence in their time of need. Make my life a reflection of Your love, and my heart a place where angles sing!"

The tape began. My friend smiled confidently, and I stepped out completely on faith. The song was perfect! Not one sign of throat problems until immediately after it was over, then my voice was completely gone again...an unmistakable witness to God's power!

The satisfaction of ministry through music was one of God's blessings for me. He had another blessing of a different kind waiting to be discovered…a wonderful, compassionate friend!

Not long after this, my sister-in-law introduced this friend to me at church on Sunday. Susan Cheney was an active witness, courageously going wherever the Lord led. We became fast friends and would drive around, go out to eat, and take exercise classes together.

Susan always seemed to know just what I needed! I remember a time when I was particularly low and she showed up at my door with a Sandy Patty tape. I listened to those songs over and over, gleaning every morsel of spiritual strength from the words.

Other times she would bring sermon tapes with excellent messages on Christian growth or suffering. I hungrily devoured each thought and scripture, seeking and finding comfort.

Susan spent many Sunday afternoons with me. This was a very hard time in the week because it used to be our time to visit with family. She kept me busy and made those tough times pass easier.

Six weeks after Kenneth's death, our wedding anniversary was approaching. I tried to put it out of my mind but that was impossible. I decided to spend February 8th with my mother rather than be alone.

About mid-morning I was in her shower washing my hair when the doorbell rang. Mother went to answer it. Suddenly, I heard her yelling for me over the sound of the water. Not taking time to rinse the shampoo out, I slipped on my robe and ran to see what was wrong. There she stood with a bouquet of roses...the same kind and color Kenneth had always sent to me on our anniversary.

I caught my breath and slowly reached for the card. *"I know it isn't the same, but I think Kenneth would have wanted you to have these today. Susan"* **2 Corinthians 1:3-4 (KJV)**

My mother and I both cried, but instead of sadness, I felt a sense of relief. The dread of the day had been wiped away by the kindness of one of God's children to another. Her Bible verses said it all: *"Blessed be God, even the Father of our Lord Jesus Christ, the Father of mercies, and the God of all comfort, Who comforteth us in all our tribulation, that we may be able to comfort them which are in any trouble, by the comfort wherewith we ourselves are comforted of God."* **2 Corinthians (KJV)**

Through her exceptional friendship, Susan enabled me to get on with my life.

Getting on with my life, at this point, meant finding a place to live. Even though Zack and I had been staying in an apartment in my brother's house, we felt we were imposing on Allen's family. The house in Knoxville meant nothing to me without Kenneth. I had decided to sell it, but there was a recession that year and real estate sales had slowed. In the meantime, I asked God to find a house I could afford until the one in Knoxville sold.

One day, Allen came home all excited, "I found the perfect house for you Evelyn. I happened to see one of our church members today at McDonald's and he told me of a house he had for sale. Since it was right next door to him, he wanted someone he knew, someone quiet to buy it. It's small, inexpensive, and in a nice neighborhood!"

Later that week I made an appointment with the real estate agent and went to see it.

The moment I walked in, I felt it was the one the Lord would have me buy, but the house just "wasn't me". I have always liked nice things, lots of interesting textures, shapes, and decorations. This house was plain with white walls, simple rooms, the basic cookie-cutter style popular at the time it was built.

I stood in the living room glumly staring at the vacant walls while the cheerful voice of the real estate agent echoed through the emptiness. As she chattered on, extolling this feature and that, I was inexplicably drawn to the front windows. Outside, the sky was sullen and overcast, matching my dismal mood. Suddenly, a shaft of brilliant sunlight burst through the dense clouds and streamed through the window as if singling out that house to receive its glory. Suspended glittering dust particles danced in the beam of light…so simple, yet, so magnificent!

"I'll take it!" The words spilled out before I could think. Soon afterwards, I understood why. With so much to be done, I could have started anew, decorating the house to reflect my tastes.

Occasionally, the Lord would give me assurances, in the minutest ways that He was in control of this move.

One time I needed some indoor-outdoor carpet for my front porch to match the brown paint on the entrance door. The salesman in the carpet store in town assured me he had nothing that color, but on my way out, I spotted it in a workroom.

"What about that?" I pointed.

"That's just where we keep scraps from our jobs." He said. "There wouldn't be anything in there big enough for what you want."

"Can we measure it?" I felt right about insisting.

To his amazement, (not mine) it was exactly the size I needed!

The house was much smaller than the one in Knoxville, but I decided to use some of my furniture from there and sell the rest. On moving day, I met the workmen early. From the very moment I entered my old house, I had a strange feeling. This once vibrant, exciting, joyful home was now cold and quiet...museum-like. Beautiful things now resting in such a dead setting. I started to get a horrible stomachache.

As each piece of furniture left the house, I felt as if I was driving another nail into Kenneth's coffin. Our marriage, our life together, hopes and dreams were over.

The stomach pains progressed and I had to lie on a bed. The movers got their instructions between moans. When they were finished, I gave them directions to the Newport house and went to the hospital, convinced I had appendicitis.

"I'm sorry, Mrs. Taylor." the doctor said after the examination. "I can't seem to find anything wrong. Could you have been under some stress lately?"

"A few months ago, my husband was killed and today I was moving out of our house. Would that have done it?"

"Yes, certainly." he said. "Get some rest and try to relax. I'll give you a prescription for a muscle relaxant." He wished me well and hurried to his next patient.

Later that evening, I met Susan for dinner and told her all that had happened at the house.

"I know **Romans 8:28 (KJV)** *"And we know that all things work together for good to them that love God…"* is true, but why is it so hard to believe?" I asked my friend.

The way to make **Romans 8:28** work is to practice **Ephesians 5:20 (KJV)** *"Giving thanks always for all things unto God and the Father in the name of our Lord Jesus Christ…"*! Susan replied. "In order for all things to work together for the good of those who love Him, you must give thanks in all things, good and bad! Prove to God you have complete trust and faith in His plan for you. Reach out to Him, touch His garment with your praise, and trust Him to work this out for your good."

When I got home that night, I thought about what Susan said. I knew in my head, she was right, but to thank God in spite of the murder of my husband went against every human instinct of my being. I looked up **Ephesians 5:20**. God's word plainly said it, and I believe His Word. I bowed my head and pushed the words past the huge lump in my throat.

"Thank you, Father, for everything in my life. I know You are in control. Thank you for…for…the good thing You will bring from Kenneth's death…."

Instead of the sadness and betrayal I thought I'd feel, all at once, I was overwhelmed with an awareness of His Presence. No, I did not feel the touch of His hand on mine, nor did I see Him, but He was there. The previously empty bedroom seemed suddenly filled with a wonderful all-enveloping benevolence and though I heard no audible voice, I knew He said to me, *"...Daughter, be of good comfort; thy faith has made thee whole." **Matthew 9:22 (KJV)***

In that scripture the woman had said, *"...If I may but touch his garment, I shall be whole." **Matthew 9:21 (KJV)*** Not only had she prayed, but had acted in faith.

It wasn't gratitude *for* Kenneth's death, but showing faith in God's control of it, that changed my whole outlook.

Kenneth's work on earth was done – but mine was just beginning. Zack needed me, and I knew my job for now was to raise and guide him to a personal knowledge of Jesus and see he got the foundation that would help him cope with any of life's challenges.

I decided right then and there to make my life a testimony of my love for God and my belief that all things *do* work together for good for those who put faith in Him.

From that time on, I really began to get my life

back together. Zack and I settled in our new home and were active in church. The Knoxville house sold the following spring to a wonderful Christian couple who seemed to understand just what that home had meant to me.

Things progressed fairly smoothly for the next couple of years until....

Chapter 8

The sudden ringing jarred me back to the present. An FBI agent leaped to the phone. As I slowly reached for my extension, he gave me a signal and we both picked up our receivers at the same time. The caller was one of many well-wishers whom I had politely but quickly dismiss so the line would be free.

I sighed and sat back down on the couch. My pastor, who had been there all night, came over and patted my hand.

"You know, Evelyn," he said, "God must have a lot of confidence in you."

"What?"

"He must know you will come through these tragedies still praising Him, still a witness to His goodness and mercy."

I just looked at him. His words really weren't penetrating my exhausted brain, but I *did* know I wouldn't fail God's test, no matter how all this turned out. He was in control. I just wished I had the patience to let Him work in His time.

The frantic activity of the agents and crushing weight of near panic, left me suffocating. I stepped outside into my backyard. The cold February night engulfed me in silent darkness. My breath came in heavy white clouds; the frosty air stung my nostrils as the wind whipped at my tears. I felt so alone.

The sides of the tall pine felt rough as I steadied myself against it. The pitch-beaded scars were still visible in the bark from Zack's "Daniel Boone" games.

"Dear God, why? Why does Kenneth have to be gone? Why do I have to handle this all by myself?"

My eyes slowly drifted upward to the clear night sky. The myriad of bright twinkling stars overwhelmed me. Suddenly, the night sky appeared as a black velvet curtain, pricked full of holes, straining to hold back all of heaven itself! Each opening gave just the amount of light needed to tempt me with a preview of the spectacular paradise behind it. I saw the true miracle of God's beautiful world!

"How can I feel alone when I have a Father who created all this? The One who knows every movement of the lowly sparrow will surely protect my small son!"

The agonizing beauty of those tiny white twinkle lights, that for the past two Christmases had brought such painful memories, now became a measure of strength. God knows our limited minds cannot possibly comprehend the whole spectacular being of Him, so He gives us His grace in tiny glittering portions.

"Thank You, Lord, for your infinite glory and wisdom delivered in such perfect measure." I whispered. "If just these small glimpses of Heavenly Light lift me on wings of peace and joy, I can't wait to see the world behind Your velvet curtain!"

I went back into the house with renewed strength because of my complete surrender into God's capable hands.

During the following hours, the *700 Club* called, then someone from Oral Robert's University, and even a complete stranger from Florida, who had seen the report on the news, to say she was praying.

I sat on the couch with Zack's picture, the corners now curled and frayed from hours of nervous caresses.

****

"Still no answer?"

"Yeah."

"What'll we do?"

The taller man shrugged. He looked over to the rumpled bed at the wide-eyed boy clad only in Winnie-the-Pooh pajamas.

"Keep tryin' I guess." he muttered.

"Things ain't going right. We gotta get a hold of the boss!"

"Shut up 'an let me think!"

Chapter 9

Valentine's Day began with bright sunlight streaming through the windows. The living room was bathed in golden highlights, burnishing the coffee table to a rich walnut. The rays danced and played merrily on Zack's colorful envelopes.

I paced from the living room to the kitchen and back, wondering why the day dared to be so beautiful while my child was missing.

The phone rang. My throat tightened.

"Hello."

"Did ya git the money?"

"Is Zack okay?"

"Yeah. I give him his breakfast. He said tell ya his "garden angel" was with 'em, and he'd said his prayers."

Tears and a sigh of relief mixed with thanks to God. There's the sign I've prayed for! Out of the mouth of this horrible man, came the confirmation I needed. Zack's alive! There was no way the kidnapper could have known about our nightly ritual, or the pet name we had for Zack's angel unless Zack were alive to tell him.

"You got the money?" he repeated urgently.

"I have some, but I can't get $200,000.00."

"Between you, your father and brothers, you kin git it!"

He gave me instructions for the switch, but strangely, asked for Burt to deliver the money, not me.

After I hung up, I looked around for Burt, but couldn't find him. I realized it had been hours since I'd seen him. The pay-off wasn't until noon. If I couldn't find him by that time, I would take the money myself.

About 9:30AM the banker brought all the money I had. It wasn't near enough. "Dear God, You are going to have to handle this. I know You turned five loaves and two fishes into enough to feed five thousand people. Please, stretch my money to satisfy these men."

I received such a sense of peace about it, I actually didn't think about the money anymore.

****

"Where *is* he?" The man slammed the phone down. "We ain't got no instructions. If he thinks we're gonna take the rap…"

"Reckon they're on to him?"

"We gotta git rid of that kid!"

"Yeah, let's dump the evidence and git outta here!"

Zack watched in terrified silence as they started toward him.

****

About 11:00AM the FBI's special phone line rang. Marta Jenkins took the call. After a few "okays" and "will dos", she hung up.

"We've got Zack." she said.

"How…wha…"

"That doesn't matter now. Get your coat. We have to go right now."

My apprehension mounted as we drove. Why wouldn't the agent tell me anything? Was Zack okay? Had he been abused?

Wanting no publicity, we took an unmarked car. One *long* half hour later we pulled around the side entrance of a motel in Kodak, a little town East of Knoxville. There were reporters waiting in the front parking lot, but for the moment, they had not noticed us.

As I entered the lobby, there, sitting on the check-in counter eating potato chips and drinking a Coke®, was that sweet little boy! He looked up at me with those big brown eyes and said, "I wanna go home."

I grabbed Zack up and held him, laughing, crying, afraid to let go!

The agents swarmed the place, looking for evidence, and asking questions. I overheard the motel owner excitedly volunteering information: "They put him out of the car and took off! I just stared at this tiny boy in pajamas and a ski mask walked across the lot toward me. That was sure a strange sight!"

The press spotted us and began to push their way into the lobby, but an agent quickly escorted Zack and me through the side door and back to the car.

Zack was quiet on the ride home. I held him tightly in my lap, looking at him as if it were the first time. The afternoon sunlight glistened in his sandy-brown hair. His little arms and legs curled snugly under the coat I had brought for him.

"Thank you, God." I sighed in relief.

When the car stopped, Zack jumped out and started running to our house like a scared dog. My brother was waiting outside. He scooped Zack up in his arms and rushed in before the photographers could take pictures.

Zack went straight to his room. He couldn't wait to take those pajamas off and get in the shower.

In the living room, my pastor and sister-in-law were waiting for me. They had strange looks on their faces.

I can't tell her." Reverend Keener said to Nancy.

They glanced uncomfortably at each other.

"What?" Their hesitation worried me.

"Evelyn," Nancy said, "it was Burt who did this."

"That's not true!" I gasped. "He's a friend. I have to go tell them they've made a mistake."

"You need to be with Zack right now." Reverend Keener stopped me. "You're exhausted from stress and a lack of sleep. Rest today and then straighten this out tomorrow." He put on his coat to leave. "Do you feel like going to church Sunday?"

"Of course I do! God's gotten us through this, and I want to publicly thank Him."

"There will be reporters there." Nancy said.

"That's right…why don't you come to the side entrance." Reverend Keener instructed.

That afternoon, the news of Zack's return began to circulate through the small town.

One of the most touching reactions happened in Zack's school. Earlier that morning, each class had cancelled their Valentine's party after they heard of Zack's abduction. About 2:00 o'clock in the afternoon the announcement came over the intercom system, "Zack has been returned home safe and sound!" Every classroom echoed with applause and squeals of happiness.

Later that day, Zack's teacher brought cards from his classmates. Mrs. Radford said with tears in her eyes that she had been as worried as I was.

"Thank you so much." I said. "I could really feel your prayers, and those of other friends, holding me up though this."

Neighbors brought cakes, the phone rang nonstop. There was a huge outpouring of love from the community. A true Valentine's Day!

Sunday morning, the press was indeed waiting for us at the front of the church, so my family whisked us around to the side entrance.

I don't know what the sermon was about that day, but I do remember it being one of the most precious services I've ever experienced. I praised God for His goodness as I gazed at the little miracle sitting beside me.

After the service, we went home with Matt and Nancy to eat lunch. When I walked in, I saw a Knoxville newspaper spread across their coffee table, with headlines: "Three Men Charged in Kidnapping Boy." The article stated, "Three Knox County males are being held in the Cocke County Jail on aggravated kidnapping charges in connection with the abduction of six-year-old Zachary Taylor...."

He (Artis) had hired both men for $25,000.00 each to kidnap young Taylor. Artis also stated that he allegedly planned the kidnapping...supplied the two men with weapons and made the reservations in an Alcoa motel where the boy was kept overnight.

"...the kidnappers' efforts to get in touch with Artis were foiled by suspicious law enforcement officers who kept a constant watch on him."

As I read the statements, my mind raced back to that horrible night. I suddenly realized Burt's harsh words, "Get what you came for and get out!" were instructions, not pleading. His nervous actions after the agent's interrogation were not out of concern for Zack, but concern for himself!

The newspaper accounts said Burt had admitted taking the phone off the hook in my office and unlocking the back door after he was inside.

How could this be? I thought he was my friend.

In the following days, there was a lot of turmoil. Reporters, interviews, friends and family hovered around.

Zack wasn't willing to tell me what happened that night. Being only six-years-old, he was confused and scared. The eyes in that sweet little face were strange— empty—as if the owner of a house had drawn the blinds and gone away.

My heart ached so desperately, wanting him to "come alive" again, to be aware of the beauty, the won-der, the fun—and, yes—even the pain of living.

"Lord," I prayed "please give my son back to me."

Weeks passed, then one night I heard Zack scream-
ing. I dashed to his bed, knelt and put my arms around
him. The tears came slowly at first, but soon he was sob-
bing his heart out.

"Mommy, I was so scared." He ventured.

"Honey, were they mean to you?" I asked.

"No, they gave me a biscuit for breakfast, but I did-
n't want it. I was cold and afraid to ask them for a blan-
ket." Then he looked up at me with those big brown eyes
and said, "I thought they killed you, Mommy."

Suddenly, I realized, the last time he saw me that
night, I was lying crumpled on the carport. He thought the
car had crushed me!

I picked up and cuddled this precious, "twice
given" gift and there, in the still of the night, I thanked
God for His protection.

When the first rays of morning sun glimmered over
the top of the East Tennessee mountains, I was still holding Zack. Sunbeams filtered into the otherwise dark
room, caressing the soft curves of Zack's little face with
pink and gold. As I looked at him, suddenly the tragedies

of my life were reduced to trivia in the light of the over-whelming sense of gratitude I felt for the blessings God had given me.

If I never become a successful singer, I already had it all. I belonged to the ONE who performs miracles, who supplies every need. My Savior, my Friend...my Light in the mourning!"

Epilogue

As I relate this story to you, I can visualize the still unopened Christmas gift from four-year-old Zack to his father. It holds such memories and has been given a place of honor on my bookshelf.

Packed safely away are other mementos from the past: the Valentines from Zack's classmates, the Winnie-the-Pooh pajamas he had worn, cards and letters from well-wishers, all serving as reminders that when tragic things happen, God is always in control: *"These things I have spoken unto you, that in me ye might have peace. In the world ye shall have tribulation: but be of good cheer; I have overcome the world." **John 16:33 (KJV)***

Sometimes we go through difficult times for a special reason. Often there's an eventual higher good to come from the experience, an important lesson for us to learn, something more important in God's plans than to have a normal family life.

No doubt these experiences have prepared me for future service to God. I believe He wants me to use the strength I've gained as a witness to His reality, and to use my voice to praise Him and bless others.

If Christians can see from my testimony, how important it is to have a close daily walk with God, then all this will be worth it. I pray any lost person who hears my story, will see the need to posses the peace and assurance God offers to His children, and will want this for themselves.

The knowledge of Jesus Christ's birth and mission on earth has intensified in my soul. Christmas is still a lonely time, but Jesus fills the emptiness in my heart.

There is a God—a living, powerful, personally involved God—who takes delight in holding off the rain long enough for me to rake leaves, or wants to be included when I make a grocery list, as well as holding me up at a loved one's funeral.

This is good news in today's troubled world. It's the same good news that Jesus shared with his disciples two thousand years ago. It's the kind of good news that's just too good to keep to myself!

I want to show, with God's help, we can become strong through the suffering we encounter, and I want others to see His grace and love in my life. I know there's a purpose for all this, and I'm willing to do whatever God asks. I have the unmistakable assurance that He will be with me, and lead me all the way home!

Evelyn

Book & Music by Evelyn Taylor-McNamara
"Light in the Mourning"
Songs

1. One Way Flight
2. Holy Ground
3. Consider the Lilies
4. When He Was On The Cross
5. It's My Desire
6. I Should Have Been Crucified
7. Love Grew Whyere the Blood Fell
8. Cups of Cold Water
9. The Only Real Peace
10. Rise and Be Healed

Order Form

QTY.   PRICE   TOTAL

_____   x $ _____   = $ _____

Shipping & Handling $2.50   ORDER TOTAL $_____

Make check payable to:

Evelyn Taylor-McNamara
PO Box 1532
Dandridge TN 37725
Shipping Instructions:

Name:_____

Address Line 1:_____

Address Line 2:_____

State:_____ Zip:_____

9 781582 752112